# SCIENCE
## in Action
### KEEPING HEALTHY

# Why do I sleep?

Angela Royston

Quarto is the authority on a wide range of topics.

Quarto educates, entertains and enriches the lives of our readers—enthusiasts and lovers of hands-on living.

www.quartoknows.com

Copyright © QED Publishing 2016

First published in the UK in 2016 by
QED Publishing
Part of The Quarto Group
The Old Brewery, 6 Blundell Street,
London, N7 9BH

A catalogue record for this book is available from the British Library.

ISBN 978 1 78493 630 3

Printed and bound in China

**Publisher:** Maxime Boucknooghe
**Editorial Director:** Victoria Garrard
**Art Director:** Miranda Snow
**Design and Editorial:** Starry Dog Books Ltd
**Consultant:** Dr Kristina Routh

**Picture credits**
(t=top, b=bottom, l=left, r=right, c=centre, fc=front cover)
**Corbis** Brigitte Sporrer/zefa/5t, Lisa B 12t, Randy Faris 12b, Heide Benser/zefa 13b, G Baden/zefa 14.
**Getty Images** Mrs_2015 fc, Steve Shott 4, Lonnie Duka 10, Kate Powers 20.
**Shutterstock** Ljupco Smokovski 6/7, JPC-PROD 7b, Juriah Mosin 8, Gladskikh Tatiana 9, VaLiza 11, Anna Tamila 12t b/g, Monkey Business Images 13t, Imcsike 15, sonya etchison 16, Tatiana Mironenko 17t, wavebreakmedia 17b, Rebecca Abell 18, Leah-Anne Thompson 19t, Monkey Business Images 19b, Karen Struthers 21t, Monkey Business Images 21b.

Words in **bold** can be found in the glossary on page 22.

# Contents

# Why do we sleep?

We sleep because we get tired. Sleeping rests our bodies, especially our muscles.

When we are really tired, our eyes want to close.

Sleep also lets our minds rest. When we are deeply asleep, we are not aware of anything.

4

After a good night's sleep, we wake up feeling refreshed and full of energy.

Children need plenty of sleep to keep them fit and healthy.

**Monday** Slept 10 hours. No dreams. Woke up by myself.

**Tuesday** Slept 11 hours. No dreams. Mum woke me up.

**Wednesday** Slept 9 hours. Had two dreams. Woke up by myself.

# Activity

Keep a diary to find out more about your sleep pattern. How many hours do you sleep? Do you have **dreams**? Do you wake up by yourself?

# Our sleeping body

When we sleep, our breathing slows down, our muscles **relax** and our **heart** beats more slowly. Our **brain** uses sleep time to sort out memories of the day. It also prepares for the next day.

Our bodies cool down a little when we are asleep.

Brain

Heart

Lungs

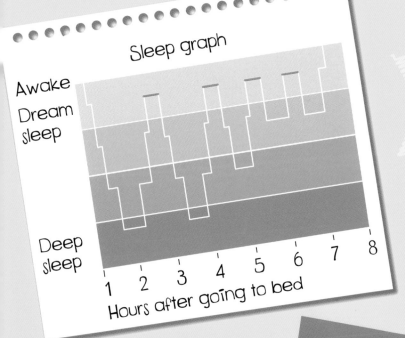

Sleep graph

Awake
Dream sleep

Deep sleep

1  2  3  4  5  6  7  8
Hours after going to bed

The way we sleep changes during the night. At first we sleep deeply, but after a few hours we sleep more lightly.

This graph shows how long we might spend in different types of sleep.

# Activity

If you find it difficult to get to sleep, try this activity in bed. Shut your eyes and breathe in and out slowly. Don't think of anything except your breathing. This will calm your mind and slow down your heartbeat.

7

# At bedtime

It's a good idea to follow the same bedtime **routine** each evening. This helps us to relax and fall asleep more quickly.

Your bedtime routine should include washing your face and brushing your teeth.

Listening to music or reading a story can help us to relax at bedtime. It's better not to play computer games or watch television. These activities can make our minds too active for sleep.

**A bedtime story can make us feel calm and cosy.**

## Activity

At bedtime, lie in bed and relax your body bit by bit. Start with your feet. Then relax your legs, followed by your stomach, arms, hands and face.

# Getting enough sleep

Most children need about 10 or 11 hours of sleep a night. Children need more sleep than adults because their minds and bodies are still growing.

We usually sleep better if our bedroom is quiet and dark.

It's a good idea to go to bed at the same time each evening. That way our brains get used to falling asleep at a particular time. Your bed will be more comfortable if it's not too full of toys.

# Activity

Try to remember a night when you stayed up very late. Did you sleep longer than usual the next morning?

Use an alarm clock to wake yourself up at the same time each morning.

Dreams are like stories that come into our minds while we are asleep. We dream about five times a night, but we usually only remember a dream if we wake up in the middle of one.

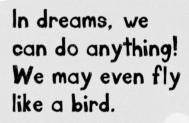

In dreams, we can do anything! We may even fly like a bird.

# Activity

Share your dreams! Think of a dream that you remember and describe it to your friend. Then listen to your friend's dream.

Dreams are often muddled and strange. They help our minds to sort out and remember things. Some dreams are nice, but bad dreams can be upsetting.

**If you have a bad dream, remember — it isn't real, and dreams stop when we wake up.**

13

# Waking up at night

People often wake up in the night. Some people find it hard to get back to sleep. If this happens to you, try to relax and let yourself fall back to sleep.

Hugging a favourite toy may help you to get back to sleep.

14

If you wake up every night to go to the toilet, try drinking less at teatime. If you wake up with a tickly cough, sipping water can help to stop the coughing.

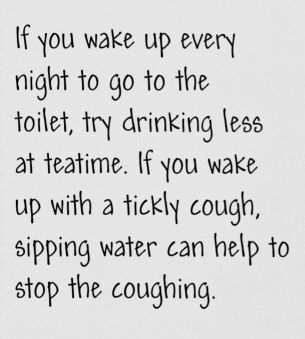

# Activity

Have you heard of 'counting sheep'? Some people count imaginary sheep to help them get back to sleep. Ask your friends what works best for them.

**Keep a drink of water by your bed in case you feel thirsty in the night.**

# Not enough sleep

If we don't get enough sleep, we feel tired the next day. We may be grumpy, too.

Yawning is the body's way of telling us that we are tired and need to sleep.

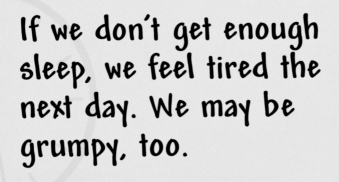

Our brains work less well when we are tired. We may learn things more slowly than usual and make more mistakes.

**If you go to school tired, you'll find it more difficult to remember things.**

# Activity

If you can't sleep at night because you are worried about something, talk to your parents or carer about what's worrying you.

# Daytime sleeping

Babies and toddlers sleep for part of the day as well as at night. They need more sleep because they are growing so quickly. Older children who get enough sleep at night should not need to sleep during the day.

Babies often fall asleep at about the same time each day.

# Activity

Some people say that yawning is catching. Test this idea by yawning loudly in front of other people. Do they start to yawn, too?

If you are ill, you may need extra sleep during the day. Sleeping helps our bodies to fight illness and get better more quickly.

When you are ill, sleep can help you to recover.

19

# Resting and relaxing

It's good to have a rest each day so you can relax. A rest helps our bodies to recover after we've been rushing around or exercising.

Resting helps us to get our breath back after exercise.

After working hard at school, relax for a while and give your mind a rest. You could play a quiet game, watch television, look at a book or listen to music.

Doing a jigsaw is quiet and relaxing.

# Activity

After eating a meal, have a rest. This lets your body digest your food. You could draw, read or just chat with friends.

# Glossary

## Brain
Our brain is inside our head and controls every part of our body. Most of the brain goes on working when we are asleep, but the part that makes us aware of what is happening around us 'switches off'.

## Dreams
We have dreams as we sleep. We see, feel and hear things that seem to be real, but are not actually happening. When we dream, our eyes flicker, even though our eyelids are shut.

## Heart
Our heart pumps blood to our lungs and around our bodies. It beats more slowly when we are asleep, except when we have an exciting dream. It beats fastest when we are most active.

## Relax
When we relax, we rest and become calmer. We relax our bodies when we rest our muscles. We relax our minds when we do something quiet and soothing.

## Routine
A routine is when we do the same things at the same time every day.

# Index

# NEXT STEPS

- Talk to your child about the importance of sleep for a healthy mind and body. Explain that sleep allows the mind to rest and recover at night. It helps the body to be energetic and alert the next day, and it also helps us to fight off germs.

- Set up a bedtime routine that your child enjoys. It could include having a bubble bath, brushing teeth and then reading a story together.

- Look for signs that a child may be short of sleep. Are they often tired during the day, or do they find it difficult to concentrate? Children vary in the amount of sleep they need, but most children aged 6 to 9 years should sleep for about 10 hours a night.

- If your child is not getting enough sleep, talk about what time they should go to bed to give them enough sleep. Try to keep to this time every night.

- If a child often wakes up at night, or has many bad dreams, try to find out what might be disturbing them. Talk to them about dreams and how they are not real. Have fun making up dreams together, in which absurd and impossible things happen.

- Talk about nocturnal animals that sleep during the day. Have fun finding out about bats and owls that hunt at night.